MARIE BARRETT

Hope
in the face of
Suicide

VERITAS

First published 1996 by
Veritas Publications
7-8 Lower Abbey Street
Dublin 1
Ireland

Reprinted 2001

Email publications@veritas.ie
Website www.veritas.ie

ISBN 1 85390 370 1

Cover illustration: Don Sutton, International Photo Library
Design: Bill Bolger
Printed in the Republic of Ireland by Paceprint Ltd, Dublin

Foreword

Thank you for picking up *Hope in the face of Suicide.*
You are welcome. Stay on and read.

> Are you tired?
> Are you lonely?
> Are you troubled or afraid?
> Have you someone to talk to?
> Did you sleep last night?
> Are you worried about today?

Whatever the reason, this book has been written for
you. Hopefully, somewhere within its pages, its feelings,
its wanting to help you, you will find words, thoughts,
ideas, that may make sense, just now, to you. Above all,
may you find a reason, a hope, the courage to go
forward, to rebuild, to restart, a little more free from
worry and guilt.

Marie Barrett
Loughrea

'Suicide'!

Has it touched you?
Has it hurt you?
Has someone you love,
who may have been unaware of your love, committed
suicide?
How has this affected you?
Has someone you know been affected by suicide –
maybe a neighbour, a work colleague, a friend?

Have you thought about suicide or are you
contemplating it at the moment? Have you survived an
attempted suicide?

Or, are you simply caring: for another, for young
people, for parents, for children, your children, your
son, your daughter, your grandchild, your
grandchildren, maybe one child, one person in
particular; for your parents, your mother, your father,
your partner, your husband, your wife, your friend; for
the elderly, the unemployed, the bereaved, the lonely,

for strangers, for students, for housewives, for mothers, for fathers, for relations, for the homeless, for anyone who may one day be touched by suicide. Whatever the reason, however you may feel, you are welcome. Do come inside. Try to feel safe. There is so much we can do – together.

Guilt is real, so is loneliness. Hopelessness is real too. The challenge sometimes is to sit with your guilt, your loneliness, your hopelessness, to acknowledge them, to welcome them, just for a little while. Denying them can make them heavier. Denying, though human, can shut out help.

Share.
Let others help you.
Believe.
Believe others want to help.
Let others in.

To begin with, let the thoughts, the feelings, the hope, the despair, the anger, the love of the meditations flow quietly over you. Follow their path gently. Try not to fight them. Ask them to shelter you, to wrap you warmly within them, to take care of you, to protect you, just now. Alone, few of us can solve life's problems. Alone, at times, life's problems may seem too big. Know that this is okay too.

For a moment, sit back.
Close your eyes.
Think out, a little more, all that is worrying you
and why.
Pick the most immediate.

What kept you awake last night?
What is keeping you awake tonight?
What is worrying you now?

Is it something within you?
Is it something, or someone?
Who or what is controlling it?
Who or what do you believe can help you?
Listen.
Listen to that need for help within.
Be silent. Be still.

Open your heart, your feelings.
Feel safe.
I am listening.
I am with you.
If you wish to, weep, cry… .
'Liquid prayers' they have been called. Know that
weeping can be a gift too.

'I never told her I loved her'; 'I never told him'; can be a heartfelt cry, especially when our loved one is no longer with us, whether dead or alive. Self-blame, self-loathing, the burden of silence. Why, oh why, did we not say it? Why? Oh Why? Today, who can hear us? Today, we may scream alone on high.

Feel it, speak it, write it. You will hear it. God will hear it. In time, your loved one will hear it too. Trust in the unknown, the unspoken. There is meeting in distance. There is meeting in loneliness. The distance of ageing, of timing, of death, of dying. The distance of youth.

'Love never says sorry', we are told.
But it does. It needs to.
'Sorry', for the silences, the unspoken feelings, the stranglehold of loving, of guilt.

'Guilt'. What do you do with it?
How do you cope with it?
'Fear'. What do you do with fear too?

Without us knowing it, and indeed sometimes always knowing it, we can live quiet lives of desperation, isolation and fear. Unspoken, they bind us tightly, strangled and broken, and ransacked inside.

> Who can we turn to?
> Where can we run to?
> Who truly knows how we may feel?
> No-one really, for 'inside is inside'.

Inside are the threads of darkness and hatred, of brightness and loving, the threads of wanting and fear.

Such is our tapestry.
Such is our make-up.
The wanting to be perfect, 'inside and out'.
The fear, the terror, that 'not perfect', may mean 'not loved'.

It is good to remember, to know, that 'the wanting to be perfect' can kill.

This is where we regain most control.
Control of our feelings,
our anger,
our hurts,
our despair,
our future,
our past.
Only in such touching can we make life real.

Denial also kills.
The denial of trust, of truth, of love.
The denial of pain.

This too is our wanting.
This too is our need.
The acknowledgement of our hurting… by others.
The acknowledgement of our path… our lives.
By those who have walked it.
By those who have shared it.
By those who may not have walked and shared it too.

The acknowledgement of the travesty of our loving,
our living,
our present,
our future,
our childhood,
our past,
our youth.
The travesty, the fear, of maybe 'no future' at all.

> All is travesty.
> All is truth.
> This is okay too.

Suicide is real. The attempt of suicide is real. Far too often does it darken our thoughts. Far, far too often, does it darken our emotions, our feelings, our families, our lives. Attempted suicide has so often been called 'the cry for help unheard'. Yet, how do we hear? And, again, we come back to truth. The truth of our feelings, the truth of love, the truth of the trauma it takes to be human, the truth of our weakness and failures; the courage to be brave, the courage to speak.

So many reasons are given for today's rise in suicide, especially among the young. Lack of faith, lack of commitment, lack of a belief, in anything, all these are quoted. Depression, unemployment, alcoholism, drug addiction, teenage pregnancy, marriage break-up, unfaithfulness, relationships, exam pressure, college pressure, life's pressure, fear of failure, in oneself or another, fear of success. These too are quoted. But, overwhelmingly, above any other reason, seems to come lack of love, lack of being loved, the fear of losing love, the hopeless, hopeless feeling of lost childhood, of lost innocence, so often through abuse; newly remembered hours and acts of betrayal, rekindled, relived in later 'flashbacks', later nightmares; hours and acts and actions that will no longer go away.

Such pain is real. Such pain cries out to be heard… by someone other than just you.
Cry out. Look for help. Disclose what is real. Be heard… now.
Try not to carry such a burden alone.
Try not to weep alone.

Such sorrow needs to be shared.
Alone, such sorrow can kill.

There is sadness in weeping.
There is sadness in crying.
But the acknowledgement of sadness is good too.
Broken and wounded, you are ready for healing.

Your heart is open now. Try to realise this.

Try to give others a chance.

Speak to them.

If they do not hear all that you are saying and feeling,
then seek those professionally or vocationally waiting to
give such help to you.

Try to understand.

Try to forgive.

But, continue your search… for you.

The 'Samaritans' come immediately to mind.

Night and day they are waiting.

Waiting for your visit, your letter, your telephone call.

Through them, or alone, work also with those
specifically trained to deal with your story, be it abuse,
rape, alcohol, gambling, childhood trauma, depression,
debt, a broken marriage or relationship, sexuality,
unemployment, bereavement, death, dying. The list
can go on and on… and it does.

There is truly someone out there specially trained to help you. Find one who is right for you.

Keep trying.
Do not give up with early disappointments.
Trust your feelings.
Find an organisation or counsellor or friend who you know can help you.

Realise that true help works towards freedom.
Towards freeing you.
Know this.
Beware of dependency creation.

In time, believe you can walk free, and in time you will.
Free with self-knowledge.
Free with forgiveness and understanding.
Free with love.
Free with truth.

Free with the permission of your own anger, your own rage. But also free from the need to carry it daily around. Such is freedom. Such is truth.

'Love one another, as I have loved you', we are told.
Now is the time to know the power of that love
FOR YOU!
Put yourself first, just now, for healing.
Put yourself first, in looking for help.
Believe in healing.
Believe there are people waiting to help you now.
Look to the unhearing and know, somewhere,
somewhere within them, they too may be hurting, for
nothing blocks our hearing like fear. The fear of what
we might hear. The fear of what we may already know
is there.

Try to reach inside the truth.
Try to look carefully at your own heart, your own home.
Truly, how is it to live with you?
Truly, how is it to be at home with you?
What do you see in your children's eyes?
Your partner's eyes?
Your eyes?
Your parent's eyes?
What lies silent, in your house, your heart, your home?

Know that all homes have their silences,
their emotional quicksands,
their feared truth.

Know that this is part of being human.
Know that this too is the tapestry of life.

Know too, that people are marvellous.
You are marvellous.
Trust.
Live.

People take so much.
People trust so much.
You already have.
Long-term you will.
Hold on.
Live.

Should you be uncomfortable with any thoughts that are now coming to you, then think deeply. Ask for guidance, inside. Go quietly and write your feelings. Let the pen 'write itself'.

Do not stop it.

Let the past and the present flow.

Let your thoughts and your feelings 'take over', on paper.

Choose beautiful paper.

Though there is pain, know that there is also beauty in truth.

Let nothing silence you. Let your heart speak.

Be silent. Be still. 'And know that I am with you' says the Lord.

Read what you have written.

Read what you have written... well.

What surprises you?

What upsets you?

How much did you already know?

Maybe not its contents, its story, but how about its feelings, its depth?

Had you known how deep,
how lonely?
Had you known how true?

This is all okay.
For love of oneself is rarely enough to bring us courage.
Rarely does it give us the strength to win the struggle to
speak.
For many, especially parents,
it is the love of and for our children, our partner,
that brings such loving, such feeling, such fear.

Be at peace. Know that you have made a beginning.
Now follow through. That is the hardest.
For the temptation now is to deny.
To deny, to diminish pain's importance.
To deny that 'all this is real'.
But 'No'!
Read back over your words.
Listen!
Cry!
Weep!
Can you really now deny how you feel?

Look up the nearest help number.
Some of these are given at the back of this book.
Others you will find in your telephone
directory or from directory enquiries.
Look also at the notices in public places, churches,
railway stations, city bill-boards. Start with the
Samaritans or any other service you may now feel is
right for you.

Make a beginning, today, if possible, but set a time
limit, possibly by the end of the week. Beginning is the
hardest. Once you have begun relief comes. Yes, there
may be tensions. Yes, there may be tears. But think
what these have already cost you! Think now what their
disappearance may bring.

A home without anger?
A home without fear?
A home without tension and dread?

A home bright with love?

A home where you can sleep at night?
A home where children can sleep?
A home to come home to?
A home safe for you?

All this is earned.
Rarely does it just happen.
Such is humanity. Such is family. Such is truth.

Don't burden your heart with perfection.
Seek the balm 'to be weak'.
Listen. Listen to your thoughts, your feelings.
Seek help.
Look for help. It is waiting.
Suicide, of oneself, of another, can be avoided.
Seek out. Speak.

Pain is real. Pain is healing.
Both are needed.
To deny this is to deny the truth of oneself.

Know that you are loved.
Know that you are needed.

Begin with self-love.
Move then to allow others to love you.
They are waiting. Believe it.

Give those around you a chance.
Let others love you.
Let others heal you.
Let others help you forgive.
Let others be forgiven.
Love and forgive yourself.

Know yourself strong, with help if necessary, in the
beginning.
For, 'when I am weak, then I am strong', St Paul has said.
Know that this is okay too.

Above all, give others a chance.
Tell your story.
Be heard, WHILE YOU ARE LIVING.
Suicide destroys not only those around you.
SUICIDE ALSO DESTROYS YOU.

Meditations

Meditation One:

I am tired.
I have nowhere to go.
I am lonely.
Make me complete.
Be with me, God.
Help me find peace.

'O that I had wings like a dove, to fly away and be at rest.'
(Psalm 54)

Meditation Two:

I am still tired.
I have no-one to turn to.
Hear me, God.
I am alone, so alone.
Help me,
Help me find peace.

'On the rock too high for me to reach, set me on high.'
(Psalm 60)

Meditation Three:

I cannot see.
I cannot hope.
What is ahead, God?
I fear.

'Lower your heavens; Touch the mountains.' Touch me.
(Psalm 143)

Meditation Four:

Thank you for today
though I am still unsure.
Where are you leading me, God?
Do you know the way?

'You, O lord, are my lamp,
My God who lightens my darkness.
With you I can break through any barrier.
With my God I can scale any wall.'
                              (Psalm 17)

Meditation Five:

Why, God?
Why?
Why me?
Why him?
Why her?
Why?
Why?
Why?
Lead me, God.
I still cannot see.
Calm the storm.
Help me find you.

'I answered, concealed in the storm cloud.'
                    (Isaiah 12:1-6)

Meditation Six:

Let me sleep gently.
I cannot.
I am still tired, God.
Help me.
I am trusting – a little.
Help me find peace.

'I trusted, even when afflicted.'
(Psalm 115)

Meditation Seven:

I hate waking,
it makes life so real.
I want to hide, God
Help me face…
this night…
this day…

'And God saw that it was good.'
                    (Genesis: 1)

34

Meditation Eight:

People are talking, God,
I can hear them.
They stop when they see me
but I still hear them.
Help me forgive.

'Be still and know that I am God.'
                    (Psalm 46)

Meditation Nine:

What is forgiveness, God?
I am still hurting.
I am angry.
Who can I turn to?
I cannot forgive.

'He will feed his flock like a shepherd,
He will gather the lambs in his arms,
He will carry them in his bosom,
And gently lead those that are with young.'
                              (Isaiah 40:10-17)

Meditation Ten:

I am happy, God,
with them,
without them.
Is that possible, God?
I am still not sure.

'We sing for you a morning hymn, to end the silence of the night.'

(Morning Prayer-Divine Office)

Meditation Eleven:

I smiled today
without feeling guilty.
I laughed today too.
Thank you, God.
I needed to.
It was good.

'I lift up my eyes to the mountains,
from whence shall come my help.'
                    (Psalm 120)

Meditation Twelve:

Life is Calvary, God.
Life is good too.
Help me find 'the middle path'.
Help me ask the way.

I am okay, God… I will be.
Life is okay, God… It will be.

I am trusting…
I am trusting… a little, God.
I trust you.
I do.

'My heart is ready, I will sing. I will sing your praise.'
(Psalm 56)

Meditation Thirteen:

Be gentle, God.
Teach me to forgive… me.
Be gentle, God.
Teach me to forgive… you.
Be gentle, God.
Teach me to forgive… them.

Lighten my heart.
Brighten my day.
Rebuild our dreams, God.
We all need you.
Be with us on our way.

'May what is false within us, before your trust give way.
That we may live untroubled, with quiet hearts this day.'
                    (Morning Prayer – Divine Office)

Meditation Fourteen:

I have courage, God.
I am trusting.
I have friends –
they are trusting too.

I have faith, God
in a tomorrow.

I am rebuilding
day by day…
night by night…

We will make it.
Be with us, God
each night…
each day…

'O God, how deep are your designs.'
(Psalm 91)

Meditation Fifteen:

I am learning, God,
learning to like me…

learning to like others…

But I have limits
of accepting…
of giving…

I have goals.
I want to succeed…

But as I am,
not as others want me to be…

I trust you, God… I TRUST ME.

'In the Evening of Life, it is on Love we shall be judged.'
(St John of the Cross)

PRAYER FOR SERENITY

God grant me
SERENITY
to accept the things I cannot change,
COURAGE
to change the things I can and
WISDOM
to know the difference.
Living one day at a time,
enjoying one moment at a time;
accepting hardship as a pathway to peace;
taking, as Jesus did, this sinful world as it is,
not as I would have it;
trusting that you will make all things right
if I surrender to your will;
so that I may be reasonably happy
in this life and supremely happy with you
forever in the next. Amen.

Reinhold Niebuhr

SUPPORT GROUPS

Aids

Aids Helpline
53 Parnell Square West, Dublin 1 Tel (01) 873 3799
Mon-Fri 7-9pm and Sat 3-5pm
Cork (021) 427 6676 Mon-Fri 10am-5pm

Alcohol

Al Anon Family Groups
5/6 Capel Street, Dublin 1 Tel (01) 873 2699
Mon-Sat 10.30am-2.30pm

Alateen
5/6 Capel Street, Dublin 1 Tel (01) 873 2699

Alcoholics Anonymous
109 South Circular Road, Leonard's Corner, Dublin 8
Tel (01) 453 8998

Battered Women

Women's Aid
Carmichael House, North Brunswick Street, Dublin 7
Tel (01) 872 5550 Freephone 1800 341900

Bereavement

Beginning Experience
St Audeon's Church, High Street, Dublin 8
Tel (01) 679 0556

Irish Stillbirth and Neonatal Death Society
Carmichael House, North Brunswick Street, Dublin 7
Tel (01) 822 4688

Bullying

National Association for Victims of Bullying
Frederick Street, Clara, Co Offaly Tel (0506) 31590

Cancer

Irish Cancer Society
5 Northumberland Road, Dublin 4
Tel (01) 668 1855 Fax (01) 668 7599 Freephone 1800 200 700

Carers

Carers Association
Metropole Centre, James Street, Kilkenny
Tel (1800) 240724

Child Abuse

Irish Society for the Prevention of Cruelty to Children
20 Molesworth Street, Dublin 2
Tel (01) 679 4944 Freephone Childline 1800 666 666

Cot Deaths

Irish Sudden Infant Death Association
Carmichael House, 4 North Brunswick Street, Dublin 7
Tel (01) 874 7007 Fax (01) 872 6056

Depression

Aware – Helping to defeat depression
Charity Shop, 147 Phibsboro Road, Dublin 7 Tel (01) 830 8449
Admin Office, 72 Lower Leeson Street, Dublin 2 Tel (01) 661 7201
Helpline Tel (01) 676 6166

Samaritans
112 Marlborough Street, Dublin 1 Tel (01) 872 7700
Reduced rate telephone line 1850 609 090

Drug Abuse

Nar-Anon
38 Gardiner Street, Dublin 1 Tel (01) 874 8431
Fellowship for those affected by another's involvement with drugs

Narcotics Anonymous
PO Box 1368, Cardiff Lane, Dublin 2
Tel (086) 862 9308 (24-hour)

Elderly

Friends of the Elderly
Little Brothers, 25 Bolton Street, Dublin 1
Tel (01) 873 1855 Fax (01) 873 1617

Gamblers

Gamblers Anonymous
Carmichael House, North Brunswick Street, Dublin 7
Tel (01) 872 1233

Homeless

Focus Ireland
14a Eustace Street, Dublin 2 Tel (01) 671 2555

Simon Community
1-2 Cope Street, Templebar, Dublin 2 Tel (01) 872 0188

Society of St Vincent de Paul
8 New Cabra Road, Dublin 7 Tel (01) 838 4164
Anglesea Terrace, Cork Tel (021) 427 0444

Threshold
Ormond Quay, Dublin 7 Tel (01) 872 6311

Trust
Bride Road, Dublin 8 Tel (01) 454 3799
Medical and social service, washing facilities

Incest

Rape Crisis Centre
70 Lower Leeson Street, Dublin 2 Tel (01) 661 4911
Freephone 24 Hour Counselling Tel 1800 778888

Loneliness

Alone
1 Willie Bermingham Place, Kilmainham Lane, Dublin 8
Tel (01) 679 1032

Marital Problems

ACCORD
All Hallows College, Dublin 9 Tel (01) 837 1151 Fax (01) 837 3207
Callsave 1890 227 427 Email admin@accord.ie

Maternity

Cúnamh/CURA
30 South Anne Street, Dublin 2 Tel (01) 671 0598
Unplanned pregnancy counselling

Miscarriage Association of Ireland
Carmichael House, 4 North Brunswick Street, Dublin 7
Tel (01) 872 2914

Poverty

Society of St Vincent de Paul
8 New Cabra Road, Dublin 7 Tel (01) 838 4164

Sexual Assault

Dublin Rape Crisis Centre (See Incest)
70 Lower Leeson Street, Dublin 2 Tel (01) 661 4911

Suicide

Friends of the Suicide Bereaved
PO Box 162, Cork Tel (021) 431 6722

Unemployment

Irish National Organisation of the Unemployed
Araby House, 8 North Richmond Street, Dublin 1
Tel (01) 856 0088 Fax (01) 856 0090

Victim Support

Irish Association for Victim Support
46 Crawford Avenue, Dublin 9 Tel (01) 860 3877